CLASSICAL TECHNIQUE
for the *Modern*
GUITARIST

Kim Perlak

To access audio visit:
www.halleonard.com/mylibrary

Enter Code
2602-5298-2412-4816

BERKLEE PRESS

Editor in Chief: Jonathan Feist
Senior Vice President of Online Learning and Continuing Education/CEO of Berklee Online: Debbie Cavalier
Assistant Vice President of Marketing and Recruitment for Berklee Online: Mike King
Dean of Continuing Education: Carin Nuernberg
Editorial Assistants: Emily Jones, Eloise Kelsey
Cover by Small Mammoth Design
Technology Consultant: Terry Taylor Barker
Photography: Jonathan Feist

ISBN 978-0-87639-167-9

Berklee Online
online.berklee.edu

1140 Boylston Street
Boston, MA 02215-3693 USA
(617) 747-2146

Visit Berklee Press Online at
www.berkleepress.com

DISTRIBUTED BY

HAL•LEONARD®
CORPORATION
7777 W. BLUEMOUND RD. P.O. BOX 13819
MILWAUKEE, WISCONSIN 53213

Visit Hal Leonard Online
www.halleonard.com

CONTENTS

ACKNOWLEDGMENTS

I am a note-taker. Through my decades of guitar education, and to this day, I've built a collection of notebooks full of assignments and advice from the masters of the instrument from whom I've been fortunate to learn. Periodically, I revisited old notebooks, photocopied them, cut out the exercises and ideas I found most relevant, and taped them into new notebooks. Eventually, my teaching method became a synthesis of these ideas.

No doubt, some guitarists who read this book will note the influence of my classical teachers: Suzanne Higgins, Judy Handler, Stephen Robinson, Benjamin Verdery, and Adam Holzman. There is an obvious presence of my classical workshop teachers Bruce Holzman, Scott Tennant, Julian Gray, Phillip de Fremery, and my colleague Steve Kostelnik (who got me hooked on ping-pong ball nails!). Also present in these pages are the players in other "fingerstyles" who collaborated with me, talked shop, taught me many things, and broadened my perspective on technique: David Hamburger, Kirby Kelley, Bret Boyer, John Knowles, Amanda Monaco, Dan Bowden, Guy Van Duser, and David Tronzo. Thank you.

Every musician who is both player and teacher knows that it's one thing to feel like you know what you're doing, and another thing to communicate that to other people. Thank you to my Berklee students in Technique Lab who helped me refine this method by asking every question from every stylistic background imaginable. A heartfelt thanks to a group of students from Austin Community College in Austin, TX, who I had the privilege of teaching while clarifying my approach. They had the passion and dedication to dive in, and the courage to tell me when I wasn't making sense—in a kind enough way to inspire me back to the drawing board. Thank you to Colton Chapman, Will Blackstock, and Josh Gilpin.

Thank you to Larry Baione (chair of the Guitar Department at Berklee) and Matt Marvuglio (dean of the Performance Division) for supporting this book. Thank you to Jonathan Feist, editor in chief of Berklee Press. And thank you to Randy Roos, recording engineer.

INTRODUCTION

On a daily basis in my work at the Berklee College of Music Guitar Department, a young player will ask, "What can classical technique do for my playing?" Classical and fingerstyle guitarists are interested in comparing my approach to what they have learned, jazz players see that this technique can help their comping and voice separation. Rock and blues players and songwriters are interested in learning classical technique for playing solo sections and accompaniments.

In my experience as a classical player with a multi-stylistic background, the concepts of our modern classical technique are relevant to players of all styles. Like me, and like many of my students and colleagues, "modern" guitarists are diverse in their stylistic pursuits—and seek a technical foundation that they can use as a base of operations.

Classical guitar technique facilitates ease of motion, efficiency, coordination, tone, control over dynamics and color, melodic connection, harmonic balance, and injury prevention. These benefits are rooted in an understanding of the hands—the way they move and the impact of these motions on expressive playing. My approach presents the concepts of classical technique, invites players to internalize the position and motions, and encourages them to explore the expressive possibilities in musical examples as they find applications in their own repertoire. Classical players will find direct applications, while players in other styles may adapt the information to honor their needs. The technical concepts remain consistent at the foundational level.

One of my early teachers, Julian Gray of the Peabody Conservatory, had this definition of a virtuoso: "A virtuoso is somebody who can do whatever they want. But they have to want to do it." For creative players, there are many valuable (and differing!) paths to a working technique. This book is a summary of the ideas I've gathered from great teachers, colleagues, and students.

I hope it helps you on your path.

Kim Perlak
Boston, MA

ABOUT THIS BOOK

Part I of this book begins with general rules, basics of posture, a discussion of right-hand fingernails, and a method for making fake nails. Part II is devoted to right-hand technical concepts, and part III focuses on the left hand. As the examples in the second section utilize the left hand as well as the right, you can cross-reference the concepts in the third section as you progress through part II.

Each technique in these sections is presented on a conceptual and practical level. The ideas behind each are explained, including: position, motion, and timing. Many of the photographs included are shot from the "player's view," what you will see when looking at your hand as you are playing. In keeping with our traditions of pedagogy, technical concepts are presented from a "right-handed" player's perspective. Guitarists who choose to play "left-handed" (fret with their right hand) can reverse the direction of the right- and left-hand designations.

The examples invite you to apply each concept in three stages:

1. By practicing and understanding the positions and motions away from the instrument

2. By practicing on open strings

3. By practicing with a composed or improvised excerpt

Ideally, you will revisit each practice stage with each technical concept in your daily practice to hone each skill and deepen your understanding. You are encouraged to write your own examples that adapt these techniques to your style, and to find excerpts in your repertoire that can serve as examples for practice. As an example of this, I have included a portion of my own practice notebook: excerpts from my transcription of "Chaconne" for lute by Sylvius Leopold Weiss (1686 to 1750). Stage 3 of each set of examples includes one of these excerpts, or one I composed based on this piece or excerpted from another Weiss piece.

While the concepts in parts II and III can be practiced independently, keep in mind that certain aspects of technique are cumulative. A fluid tremolo, for example, is dependent on a working right-hand position. In part IV, I've provided suggestions for organizing the examples into short warm-up routines that you can incorporate into your daily practice sessions. Part IV also includes my entire transcription of "Chaconne" by Weiss.

THE RECORDINGS

The recordings serve as audio references to guide your practice, and starting places as you develop and compile your own examples for practice. To access the accompanying audio, go to www.halleonard.com/mylibrary and enter the code found on the first page of this book. This will grant you instant access to every example. Examples with accompanying audio are marked with an audio icon.

PART I

Starting Points

GENERAL RULES

Classical technique is based on an understanding of the hands' anatomy. From this foundation, you will be able to play with maximum facility and expression, and with minimal risk of injury. In general, as a student of the modern classical technique, you will follow these rules:

1. Position your body in a relaxed, comfortable, and stable posture.

2. Consider using nails on your right-hand fingers, and understand the way the shape of your nails affects your tone and facility. Nails or no nails, you will find a "contact point" for the string on each fingertip that will provide you with consistency in your sound.

3. In your wrist position, with both right and left hands, avoid right angles, maintaining a slight outward curve.

4. When playing the strings with the right-hand fingers, play into your hand from the big knuckle.

5. In rapid scale or arpeggio passages, coordinate the timing of your right-hand fingers so that one motion sets up the next motion.

6. Practice specifically to achieve the coordination of the right- and left-hand fingers.

7. View your technique as a tool for expression, using your practice to determine the ways in which weight on the string, speed of attack, positioning, and follow-through create the sounds you desire in each technical concept.

8. Practice slowly, developing an understanding of each concept, and repeating the motions at a speed that allows for relaxed and expressive execution.

POSTURE

The most obvious difference in posture with guitarists of different styles is that classical guitarists remain seated with the instrument on the raised left leg, while traditional or popular-style players generally place it on the right leg or stand and use a strap. Both positions will work with classical technique as long as the following guidelines are observed.

The upper bout of the guitar's body should be central to your chest at the breastbone. This allows the shoulders to relax and remain level without hunching, and it allows both arms to find their position comfortably. The guitar is positioned at the appropriate height by raising the leg on which the instrument rests. Most players use an adjustable footstool for this purpose. Both feet should be flat for optimum balance, and the small of the back should be straight. If you are seated with the instrument on your left leg, the guitar is tilted slightly away from your chest on a diagonal to keep the back of the instrument from being muted by your body, and so that you can better see the fingerboard.

If you are seated with the instrument on your right leg, twist to the right from your waist in order to give your right hand and arm free access to the upper positions of the guitar neck without running into the torso.

The guitar should contact your body for balance in three places: on the leg, at the breastbone, and at the right forearm. The main variable is the angle of the guitar neck. Shorter players tend to keep the neck fairly horizontal, while taller players tend to position the neck on a steeper angle. The general rule is that the head of the guitar should not be higher than the player's head. This would negatively affect the angle of the left hand. Standing players can modify the height and angle of the instrument with the strap.

(a)   (b)

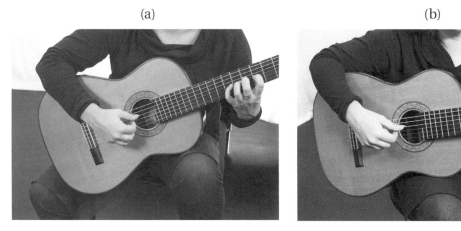

FIG. I.1. Guitar Position (a) Resting on Left Leg (b) Resting on Right Leg

YOUR "CONTACT POINT" AND THE QUESTION OF "NAILS OR NO NAILS?"

In any kind of fingerstyle playing, your right-hand contact point—the precise place that your fingertip contacts the string— is the key to your tone and your volume. When you find your contact point, you'll be playing off the same place on each fingertip on every stroke, providing you with a consistent tone. As you learn to control your dynamics and attacks, you'll be adding or subtracting weight from your contact point.

In the modern classical tradition, guitarists grow and shape the nails on their right-hand fingers. When playing with nails, the contact point is on the flesh and the nail together—*not* on the nail alone. The combination of finger and nail contacting the string at the same time will give your tone a warm fullness (from the soft fingertip) and clarity (from the hard nail). The shape of your nail serves two purposes:

1. It focuses your contact point to one small area of your fingertip, providing consistency in your sound, and

2. It acts as a ramp for the strings as your finger plays, facilitating speed.

Nails became common practice for concert classical players during the late nineteenth century, and using them is standard in the modern classical guitar community. Many fingerstyle acoustic and electric guitarists also use nails, citing the same benefits in tone and facility.

Throughout our guitar communities, there are many players who decide not to use nails, and instead contact the string solely on the flesh of their fingertips. In the classical community, these players continue in the "pre-nail" nineteenth-century tradition. For some players in other styles, nails can be problematic, interfering with hybrid picking, percussive playing, breaking on heavy-gauge strings, or adding a brilliance in tone that is not desired.

Nails or no nails, you will have to practice slowly and with awareness to establish your contact point and refine your tone.

No Nails

If you choose *not* to grow nails, you'll have to find a precise contact point on your right-hand fingertips. Nail players will shape their nails to direct the contact point on each finger. Without nails, a much larger area of the fingertip is available to the string. If the contact point is not precise, the fingertip will get stuck—cutting down on your facility, and your tone will be inconsistent. No-nail players commonly position their right hand so that they can choose a corner of their fingertip as a contact point. A common method is to direct your contact point on the thumb-side corner of each fingertip.

You will develop callouses on your fingertips if you play without nails, and you'll have to file them from time to time to keep your tone consistent. No-nail nylon string players often use gut or synthetic-gut strings because the trebles are wound. This makes them less slippery for the fingertip.

Nails

If you *do* choose to grow nails, the shape and care of them is key. Remember, you will contact the string with the flesh of the fingertip *and* the nail. Do not play with the nail alone, and do not place the string between the fingernail and the fingertip. If you do so, your tone will be thin and inconsistent, and you will get stuck on the strings as you play. The shape, length, and smoothness of your nails will affect your tone and your facility. It will be important for you to maintain them.

SHAPE

Nail players have differing opinions about ideal nail shape, and spend time experimenting to find the best shape for their playing style. You can begin with the most common basic shape and modify it based on what you need. Using a nail file, shape each nail in a 45-degree angle-ramp with the high point on the pinky-side of the fingertip.

FIG. I.2. Nail Angle Ramp: 45 Degrees

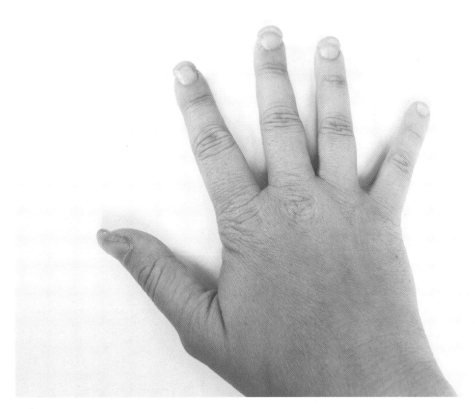

FIG. I.3. Full Set of Nails

This shape works the best for the common right-hand finger motion, the "free-stroke," and creates a full tone by directing the weight of the hand towards the soundboard. Rounding the edges of the ramp will give you a rounder tone. Keep the high point of the ramp on the pinky side of the nail; if it is in the middle, you will get stuck on the string. The exact placement of this high point may be different for each finger. This, and the overall length of your nails, will be subject to refinement as you progress through your development.

To find your contact point, place your finger on the string so that the string is sitting on the flesh of your fingertip, but also touching the nail.

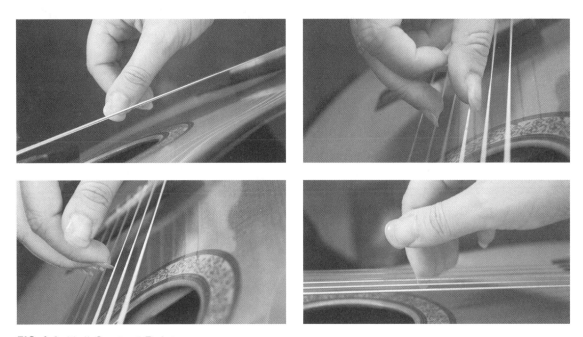

FIG. I.4. Nail Contact Points

CARE

In caring for your nails, you'll need a file to create the shape and a buffer or fine-grade sandpaper to smooth out any nicks, dings, or inconsistency in your ramp. Many players choose a metal file and use only the smoother side to make the shape. The nail must be smoothed at that point either with a buffer or with fine-grade sandpaper.

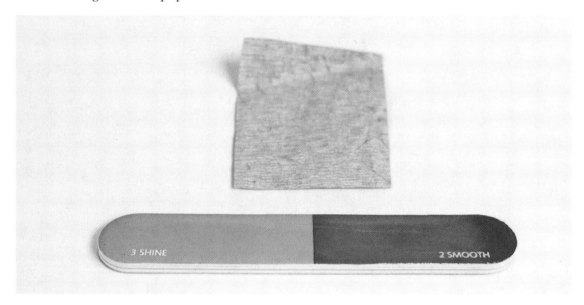

FIG. I.5. Sandpaper and Buffer

If this is the first time you're purchasing sandpaper for this purpose, I suggest that you do so from a guitar shop or teacher to make sure the grade is fine enough. Sand or buff your nails every day before and after you practice. They will break or rip less, and your tone will maintain its clarity. This is especially important for steel-string or electric players because steel strings will tear up fingernails faster than nylon strings. When using the sandpaper, put the edge under the nail, and really work it in with your left hand. After sanding or buffing, run the ramp of each right-hand nail over the pad of your left-hand thumb so you can feel that your nails are smooth.

NAIL REPAIR

If you do develop a nick, break, or tear, *don't* cut the nail off. Instead, find a porous material—like a tea bag, a ribbon, or even toilet paper will do in a pinch—and some Super Glue. Place a tiny square of whatever you choose over the crack, and then completely soak it with Super Glue. When it dries, it will bind the crack, and you can file it down smooth. Even a crack at the quick of the nail will grow out in a few weeks.

If your nails dip in the middle as they grow, or grow out wavy or bowed, the 45-degree angle shape should help. Make sure that when you put your file against the nail, it touches at all points (see figure I.2).

If you want to get a dip out, you can use the "hot spoon" method. First, place a cold spoon over the fingertip to protect it. Then, heat up the edge of a second spoon using a hot plate. Place the hot spoon underneath the nail (but over the cold spoon). The heat will melt your nail. Reshape your nail using the spoon, and as your nail cools, it will harden in the new shape. You'll have to repeat this process about once a week.

FAKE NAILS

Many players use fake nails instead of their real nails for better consistency or for added strength. There are several options, each with advantages and drawbacks in terms of reliability, labor, and the effects of the materials used on tone production. Options include acrylic nails put on in a salon and glue-on nails you can purchase in a beauty supply store or from guitar mail-order services. Similar to the repair method, you can layer silk wrap on top of your own nail and glue it in place to reinforce your nail. You can make fake nails out of ping-pong balls and Super Glue them underneath your own shortened nail.

Ping-Pong Balls

After many years of wearing down my natural nails on my bass strings and fearing the potential havoc steel strings could wreak, I began using "pongs." In developing my method, I had great teachers who had mastered this technique and have beautiful sounds on the instrument. Over the years, many players have asked me about this largely oral tradition. Here are the steps that work for me.

Get the right ping-pong ball. The "right" ball is the one made of the most dense, thick plastic you can find. If you use a thin ping-pong ball, the Super Glue will eat away at the plastic before the seal is made with your nail, compromising the seal and softening the plastic. There is a chemical spray (available in nail salons) that you can use to accelerate the fusing process, but with a high-quality ping-pong ball, this is not necessary. I have the best luck with the Nittaku 3-Star Premium from Japan, and I find that the orange balls work better. These can be ordered by mail. One ball yields two to four sets of nails, depending on the size of your fingers.

FIG. I.6. Ping-Pong Ball

1. Get the right tools. You need Super Glue (or any brand), nail clippers, scissors, a rough file, and buffer or sandpaper.

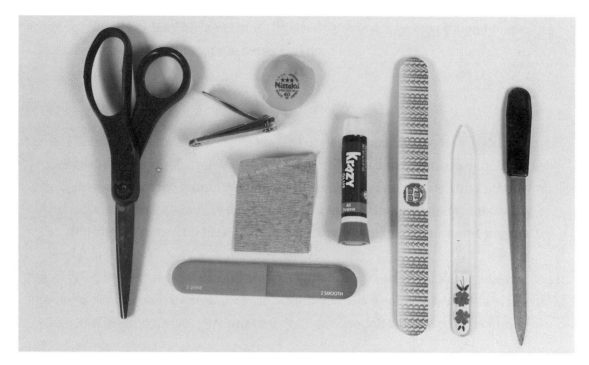

FIG. I.7. Nail Care Tools

2. Pierce the ball with the pointy tool on the nail clippers. Insert the scissors and cut the ball in half. Cut out a rectangle a little wider than the width of the nail on which you're working, and taller than you'd like in the end. Then cut a half-moon shape into this square in the shape of your cuticle.

FIG. I.8. Half-Moon Shape Cut into Ping-Pong Ball

3. File your nail down, leaving enough real nail to support the ping-pong nail.

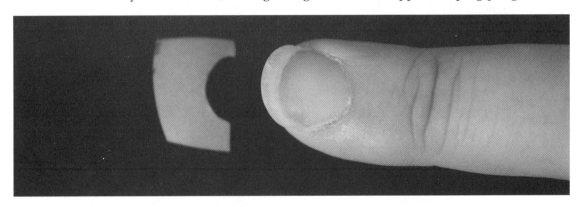

FIG. I.9. Filed Down Nail and Prepared Fake Nail

4. Put a line of glue on the half moon of the ping-pong ball.

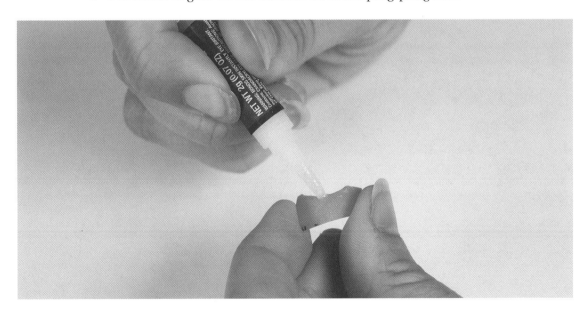

FIG. I.10. Gluing the Fake Nail's Half-Moon Curve

5. Press the ping-pong nail under your real nail, and hold it there until the seal forms (less than a minute).

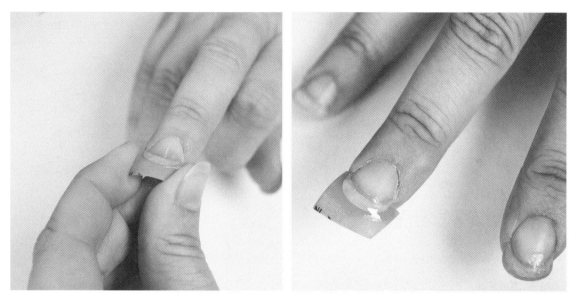

FIG. I.11. Gluing On the Square

6. Put another line of glue on top of the seal.
7. When the glue is completely dry, use nail clippers to clip a rough shape.

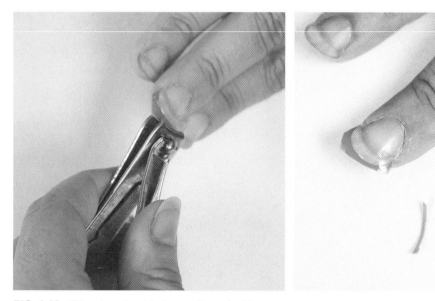

FIG. I.12. Clipping the Nail to a Rough Shape

8. Use the rough file to create the 45-degree angle shape.

FIG. I.13. Filing Down to 45-Degree Angle

9. Use the buffer or the sandpaper to make the nail smooth. Don't forget the top of the nail.

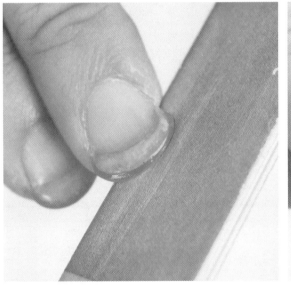 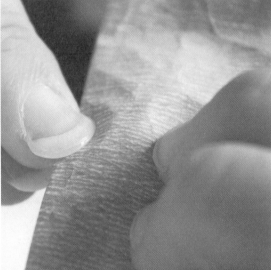

FIG. I.14. Buffer and Sandpaper

Your finished product!

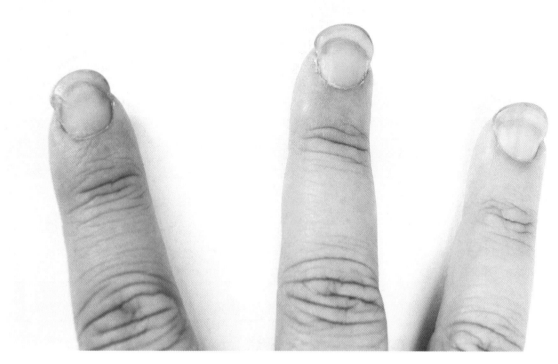

FIG. I.15. Finished Nails

PART II

Right-Hand Technique

In this book, we will use the standard *p-i-m-a-c* abbreviations for right-hand fingering:

p   thumb

i   index

m   middle

a   ring

c   pinky

BASIC ARM AND HAND POSITION

Before thinking about your hand position, consider the way your right arm is positioned on the guitar. Classical guitarists who rest the instrument on their left leg tend to contact the instrument with their right arm just below the elbow at the base of the forearm. Electric players, especially those with a "Strat-style" tapered body, generally do the same. Steel-string players and hollow-body jazz players, whose instruments generally have wider bodies at the lower bout, rest their right arms on the body of the guitar at the elbow. Classical guitarists produce their fullest sound by positioning the right hand behind the sound hole (over the "soundboard"). For the same sound quality, steel-string guitarists position their right hand *over* the sound hole.

With these parameters in mind, place your right arm on the body of the guitar, and let your hand fall into the position of a loose fist, resting *p* on the fourth string, *i* on the third, *m* on the second, and *a* on the first. Your little finger, *c*, should be loosely curled in your hand without tension. (While some classical players develop their *c* finger as a playing finger, that technique is not part of this method.) You want your fingers to pluck the strings on a diagonal—*not* straight on, which would be perpendicular (which produces a thin tone), *or* parallel (which produces a muffled, muddy tone).

FIG. II.1. Right-Hand Position

To develop your basic hand position further, consider that there are three wrist motions that make a difference: angle, height, and tilt. To internalize these motions, take your right hand off the guitar, and then follow these directions.

1. **Angle.** To experiment with "angle," move your right hand from side to side at the wrist joint. In the classical technique, your goal is to play with no angle, what players refer to as a "straight wrist." When your wrist is positioned with no angle, you could draw a straight line from your elbow through your middle finger. Playing with a straight wrist does two things: (1) It alleviates pressure caused by angling the wrist joint, which causes tension in your forearm and can lead to injury, and (2) It allows you to use the full weight of your arm in your stroke, increasing your dynamic range. Many players perform beautifully with wrists angled to the right. If you are one of them and feel tension or wish for louder dynamics, experiment with a straight wrist to feel the difference. There may be moments for adaptation or application of this technique in your repertoire.

2. **Height.** To get a sense of "height," bend your wrist up and down. Height in your wrist refers to the position of your wrist joint in relationship to your big knuckle. Pull your wrist "up" so that it is level with or on a slightly higher diagonal than your big knuckle. This amount of height will allow you to pull your fingers back into your hand from the big knuckle, as if you're making a fist. With enough height, your fingers can move through the strings diagonally, putting weight through their contact points into the soundboard. With too little height, your wrist and fingers with have to move up and away from the strings as you play, resulting in a percussive, thinner sound. With too much height, you'll lose power, and you'll find it difficult to play with a full stroke through

the string. For those of you who are required by style to palm mute or create percussion by pulling the strings up, you can deviate to do so. The higher wrist can be your basic position, and you can lower it when you need to.

3. **Tilt.** To try "tilt," make a straight wrist and rotate your entire forearm with your hand, as if you're turning a doorknob. Because the thumb side of the hand is heavier, your tendency will be to tilt your hand and arm towards the thumb side, but don't. Tilt slightly away from the thumb. This will support your weaker fingers as they are playing and give you a clean, consistent tone.

Once these three motions make sense to you away from the guitar, pick up your instrument, and place your hand in the basic position. Now, consider your angle. Next, your height. Then, your tilt. Consider your contact point on each finger, making sure, if you are using nails, that the string is touching both the finger and the nail. Take your hand off of the guitar and put it back into position as many times as necessary to internalize the position and make it work for you.

(a)   (b)

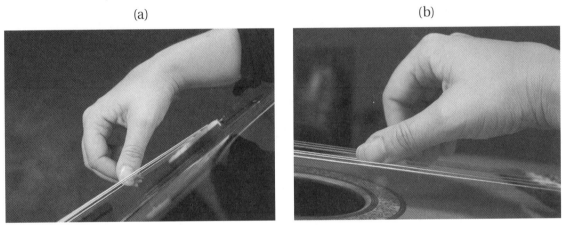

FIG. II.2. Right-Hand Position: Player's Perspective

TONE, ARTICULATION, AND A NOTE ON TIMING

As stated in part I, classical guitarists control tone and dynamics with two things in the right hand: (1) the contact point, and (2) the amount of "weight" (literally, the weight of your hand) that you apply to the string before you play it.

Once these are in place, you can further manipulate your tone by changing the tightness or looseness of your tip joints, the speed of your attack, the placement of the hand closer to the bridge (giving you a bright, ponticello tone), over the sound hole (giving you a full tone), or over the neck (giving you a dark, tasto tone), and with the shape of the fingernails. Placing the thumb/finger on the string at the contact point is known as "planting," also referred to as a "preparation." For short, staccato articulations, plant your thumb sooner on the string. For longer, tenuto articulations, delay your planting and push p through the string with a slower follow-through.

Speed, evenness, and facility in scale or arpeggio playing are issues of timing. In the classical technique, each concept that involves more than one motion requires this understanding.

As each technical concept is introduced, you will be encouraged to explore your tone and timing in the musical examples.

THE THUMB

Physically, the thumb (*p*) is the hand's heaviest appendage, so it's a good place to start. The thumb "plays" from the point at which its bone connects with the wrist.

Away from the guitar, put your hand and wrist into position and lift up your thumb. Now, let it fall as dead weight on to the tip joint of your index finger. Repeat this motion. These "thumb push-ups" will help your hand internalize the motion.

Pick up your instrument, and put your hand in position. While *p* plays, rest *i*, *m*, and *a* on the treble strings for balance. Remember, eventually you want your fingers to work together, so stay in a relaxed position as you practice your thumb.

Place *p* on the fourth string. Find your contact point on the edge of your fingertip and on your nail (if applicable). Feel the weight of your thumb on your contact point. The amount of weight you apply to your contact point when you plant will determine your volume. For example, a small amount of weight will produce a soft dynamic. Choose your dynamic. Plant, play the note, and let *p* "follow through." This means that your thumb will become dead weight, and you will let it fall on the tip joint of your index finger, which is resting on the third string.

(a)   (b)

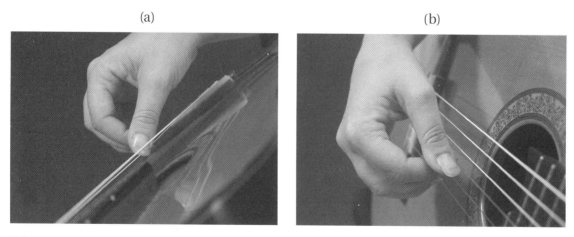

FIG. II.3. Thumb Contact Point: On String and Follow-Through

Practice

Away from the Guitar

Practice "thumb push-ups," as explained on page 16.

On Open Strings

Play the fourth string several times, establishing three different dynamic levels (soft = *p*, medium = *mf*, and loud = *f*). Repeat this on strings ⑤ and ⑥. Practice this example at each dynamic level with ponticello and tasto tone colors, and staccato and legato articulations.

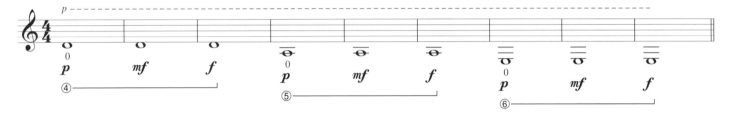

FIG. II.4. Thumb on Open Strings

To establish distance between the strings for your thumb, play the strings in the following order: ⑥,⑤,④,⑤. Repeat, establishing three dynamic levels, and experimenting with tone colors and articulations.

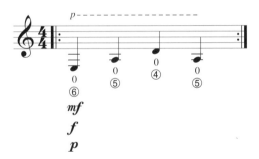

FIG. II.5. Thumb on Alternating Bass Strings

With the Left Hand

Play this one-octave A minor scale on the bass strings. Pay attention to the timing of your left-hand fingers and your thumb. Incorporate a crescendo as you ascend the scale and a decrescendo as you descend. Repeat the example, changing your articulation. (See also part III: Left-Hand Position, Coordination.)

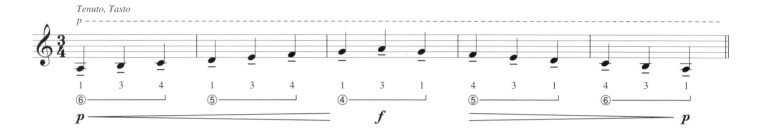

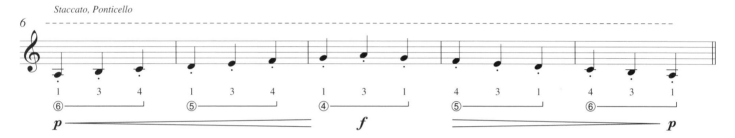

FIG. II.6. Thumb with One-Octave Scale

Composed Examples

1

Practice this melody, which stays on the fourth string. Choose your dynamics, colors, and articulations, and practice them until they feel and sound natural and expressive. (Write them in!)

FIG. II.7. Thumb on One-String Melodic Excerpt

Practice this melody, which changes from the fourth to fifth strings and back to the fourth. Choose your dynamics, tone colors, and articulations, and practice them until they feel and sound natural and expressive.

FIG. II.8. Thumb on Two-String Melodic Excerpt

THE FINGERS (*i, m, a*)

Free Stroke

In "free stroke," the staple of right-hand playing, the fingers play the strings on a diagonal, moving from the big knuckle, and following through into the palm of your hand.

To try this away from the guitar, put your hand in position. Play your fingers back into your hand from the big knuckle, making a loose fist, with the goal of touching your palm with your fingertips. You will relax this follow-through as you play on the instrument—not touching your palm each time. While away from the instrument, this motion will teach your fingers to move from the big knuckle and not the mid-joint. Make sure you allow c to follow through with your playing fingers!

Now, pick up the instrument. Plant your thumb on the fourth string for balance and plant *i*, *m*, and *a* on the treble strings. Make one more adjustment to your position: bring your hand "over the strings." This means that the big knuckle of each finger should be over the string that it is playing. This will aid in your follow-through and add power to your stroke. Apply your desired amount of weight, and play all three fingers at once. As you follow through, make sure your fingers are relaxed.

(a) (b)

FIG. II.9. Free Stroke (*i-m-a*) and Follow-Through

When playing one finger at a time, plant *p* for balance, and plant *only* the finger that will be playing. This will add power to your tone and allow your hand to fully relax on the follow-through. Fingerstyle players who play slide often plant their other right-hand fingers while playing single fingers for purposes of muting. If this applies to you, experiment with the technique presented here and feel the effect. There may be aspects of tension release and tone production you can adapt as you go back to your muting technique.

Practice

Away from the Guitar

Practice *i*, *m*, and *a* together, as explained in the preceding text above. Move from the big knuckle and touch your palm on your follow-through.

On Open Strings

Practice the fingers individually and together, taking care to follow through after you play. Keep your thumb planted on the fourth string for balance, but do not plant your fingers if they are not playing.

Practice playing at three distinctly different dynamic levels, and practice both staccato and tenuto articulations, and ponticello and tasto colors.

FIG. II.10. Free Stroke on Single Open Strings

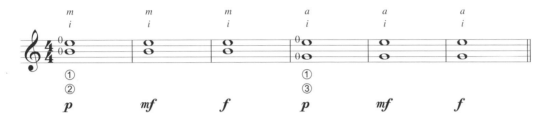

FIG. II.11. Right-Hand Fingers in Pairs

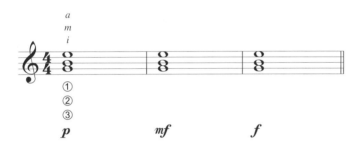

FIG. II.12. *a-m-i* Together

Composed Example

Practice this melodic example harmonized in thirds and sixths, taken from "Passacaglia" by S.L. Weiss. As you practice, pay attention to the phrasing of the line. Focus on bringing out the high voice and connecting both lines.

FIG. II.13. Musical Excerpt Right-Hand Fingers in Pairs

Rest Stroke

In a rest stroke, you'll deviate from your basic hand position so that you can extend your finger, allowing it to follow through on to the string behind the one it's playing. This technique is used as an occasional loud, full dynamic, in scale playing with *i* and *m*, or with *a* to bring out a melody line in an arpeggiated passage. This technique allows your fingers to push the string into the soundboard with more weight, but because it requires a change in hand position, you'll use it sparingly.

To set up for rest stroke, put your hand in the basic position. Plant your thumb on the fifth string. Tilt your wrist and forearm towards your thumb. Extend the finger that is playing, and find your contact point on the fingertip and the low point of the nail's ramp. Instead of positioning your big knuckle "over the strings," place this joint one or two strings behind the one you are playing. This should happen naturally when you extend your finger. When you follow through, rest your finger on the string behind the one it has played.

(a)   (b)

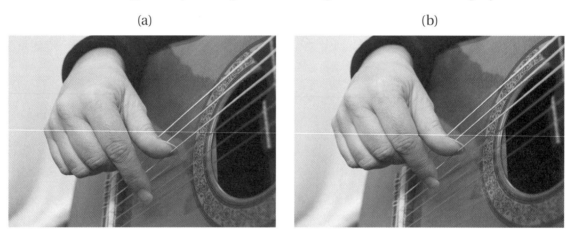

FIG. II.14. Rest Stroke

Practice

To begin practicing the rest stroke technique, use the following example.

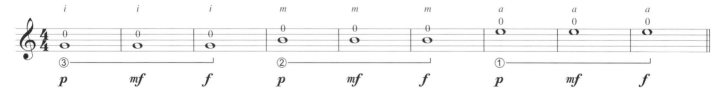

FIG. II.15. Rest Stroke on Open Strings

CHORDS: *p-i-m-a* TOGETHER

When you are playing chords or dyads—four, three, or two notes together using a combination of thumb and fingers—remember that the techniques for *p* and free stroke fingers apply. Play the fingers as they are supposed to be played (free stroke) with the proper follow-through, and the thumb in its proper technique with the proper follow-through. This means that the thumb will follow through on the *outside* of *i*—not inside the hand. If your fingers follow through back into your hand, your hand will not "bounce," or move up and away from the strings as you play.

Place your hand in position, with *p*, *i*, *m*, and *a* planted on the top four strings, and play them together. As the motion becomes comfortable and your tone becomes clear, focus your ear on the first string note. Don't try to apply more weight, but sing the note and try to hear it louder in your ear. This focus tells your *a* finger to apply just enough weight to bring out that note. Try this with *p*, *i*, and *m* as you practice the examples.

Practice

Away from the Guitar

Place your hand in position, and then "play" your fingers and your thumb at the same time. Make sure you relax on the follow-through.

On Open Strings

Practice these examples, following the "Away from the Guitar" directions. Practice playing at three distinctly different dynamic levels with ponticello and tasto colors, and practice both staccato and tenuto articulations.

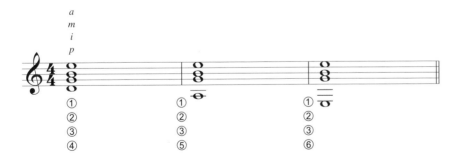

FIG. II.16. Chords on Open Strings with Alternating Bass

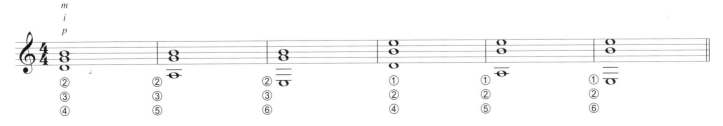

FIG. II.17. Chords on Open Strings on Different String Sets

4

Composed Example

Practice this example, which outlines the harmony in the "Theme" of "Chaconne" by S.L. Weiss. Concentrate your ear on the top, melody line to bring it out over the chords.

FIG. II.18. Chord Excerpt

TIMING

From here on, the discussion of right-hand technique focuses on timing in scales and arpeggios. (In classical technique, "arpeggio" describes a fingerpicking pattern, not a succession of chord tones in ascending or descending order.) In scale and arpeggio playing, the way you set up your motions determines your facility and allows you to play the notes evenly. This approach allows you to consider the timing of each technique first—developing your muscle memory—before you negotiate the spacing and the tension of the strings. As with the sections that covered basic position and strokes, the next sections will include examples to "play" away from the instrument. The more you revisit the basics in your practice without the instrument in your hands, the more you will internalize these technical concepts.

ALTERNATION (SCALE TECHNIQUE)

In classical technique, "alternation" is the equivalent of "alternate picking" in popular and traditional styles. Two fingers are used alternately to play a scale or a melody. Here's how the timing works: as one finger plays, the next finger kicks out of the hand, setting up to play the next note. The most commonly used alternation is between *m and i*. These are the two strongest fingers in the hand, and they are each controlled by different tendons. This makes the alternation stronger than with any other combination.

(a)   (b)

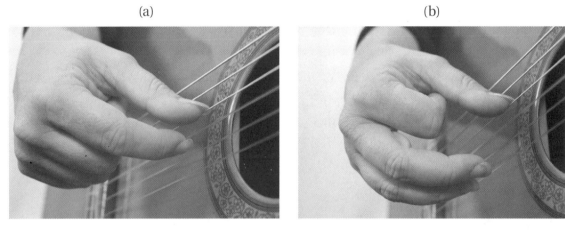

FIG. II.19. Free Stroke Alternation of *i* and *m*

(a)   (b)

FIG. II.20. Rest Stroke Alternation of *i* and *m*

Remember, you will plant your finger on the string on its contact point and apply your desired amount of weight *before* you play; don't just hit the string. As your contact point and awareness of weight become part of your muscle memory, this part of your stroke will become automatic. You'll continue to practice slowly and consciously every day to refine and reinforce this essential technical component.

Practice

Away from the Guitar

1. To establish your timing, relax your hand, keeping your wrist straight and letting your hand hang in a slightly curved position. "Play" your *i* finger from the big knuckle into your palm with full follow-through, simultaneously kicking out *m*, *a*, and *c*. Then, "play" those fingers, simultaneously kicking out *i*. Notice that *m*, *a*, and *c* naturally follow through together. They are connected in your hand. It is most efficient to honor that by allowing them to move together when possible, and refingering scale passages that alternate *m* and *a*.

2. To add some resistance and better simulate playing away from the instrument, support your elbow, and place your hand in position so that your fingers are "playing" a soft surface—like a pillow or your leg. Plant your thumb on this surface as it would touch the fourth string, and "play" your *i* and *m* alternation. The sound created will help you assess your timing.

On Open Strings

Practice alternating *i* and *m*. Play *i* on the third string, *m* on the second string, making sure to prepare/plant and follow through. Plant *p* on the fourth string for balance when using free stroke and on the fifth string when using rest stroke. Next, practice alternating *i* and *a*. Play *i* on the third string and *a* on the first string. Apply tone colors, dynamics, and articulations. Practice both free-stroke and rest-stroke techniques.

FIG. II.21. Alternation on Open Strings

On an Open String

Now, alternate both pairs of fingers on the open third string, keeping your thumb planted on the fourth string during free stroke and on the fifth string during rest stroke.

FIG. II.22. Alternation on a Single Open String

Composed Example

Practice this melody from the "Theme" of "Chaconne" by S.L. Weiss, fingered on the second string. Choose your dynamics, tone colors, and articulations. Practice both free-stroke and rest-stroke techniques.

FIG. II.23. Alternation on a Single-String Melodic Excerpt

STRING CROSSING: SCALES AND SINGLE-LINE MELODIES

Free-Stroke String Crossing

Scales and melodic lines rarely stay on one string. Therefore, you have to practice crossing strings while maintaining your hand position. Many players make the mistake of keeping their hand still and reaching for higher strings as they ascend in a scale, but this forces your fingers to play more from the mid-joint (losing power), it lowers your wrist (compromising your follow-through), and it disrupts your contact point (changing your tone).

There are two common classical techniques for string crossing, and we'll start with the most common approach. First, place your hand in position with *p* planted on the fourth string, ready to alternate *i* and *m* on the third string. Using the elbow as a fulcrum, drop your hand and arm across the strings diagonally so that *p* plants on the third string, and *i* and *m* move into position to alternate on the second string. Repeat this process, ascending to the first string, and then descend the strings one by one, following one string behind with your thumb. Do this without angling your wrist and while keeping your hand consistent in its basic position. When you get to the bass strings, you'll have to slightly angle your wrist to the right (the only time you bend that joint) so that you won't sound "scratchy" on the wound strings. As you string cross from the bass strings to the treble, straighten your wrist again back into your basic position. When playing a scale, your thumb will generally follow one string behind your alternating fingers. In melodic lines, you can modify this as necessary, planting the thumb on a lower string. The closer the thumb is to your alternating fingers, the more stable your hand.

(a)   (b)

FIG. II.24. Free-Stroke String-Crossing Technique 1: Beginning and End Points

At first, you may find the diagonal motion of this string-crossing technique extreme and worry that moving toward the bridge as you ascend will affect your tone color. With practice, your diagonal motion will become subtle and the change in tone color will be minimal.

A second way classical players maintain hand position while string crossing is by sliding their right arm back across the body of the instrument towards their torso as they descend the strings, and sliding it over the body of the instrument as they ascend. Some players find that this technique allows them to be faster in their descending scales. This approach is less common because it causes your arm to leave its position. If you adopt this technique, you will have to regain your arm position after each scale or single-line passage. As with the first string-crossing technique, allow *p* to follow one string behind your alternating fingers for stability.

(a)   (b)

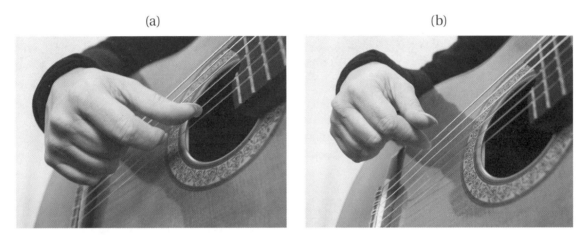

FIG. II.25. Free-Stroke String-Crossing Technique 2: Beginning and End Points

Rest-Stroke String Crossing

Rest-stroke string crossing can be performed with either string-crossing technique. Follow the same steps you practice with free stroke, but with rest stroke, *p* will follow your alternating fingers two strings behind.

(a)   (b)

FIG. II.26. Rest-Stroke String-Crossing Technique 1: Beginning and End Points

(a)   (b)

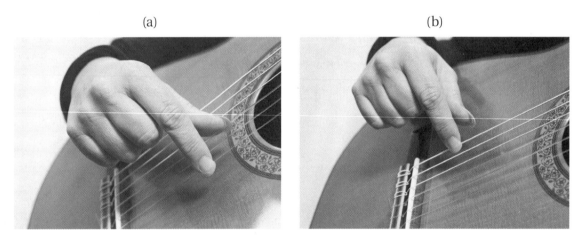

FIG. II.27. Rest-Stroke String-Crossing Technique 2: Beginning and End Points

Practice

On Open Strings

Play four notes on each open string, alternating and consciously watching your hand position as you cross strings. Use: *i-m* alternation and *i-a* alternation. Use the techniques of both free and rest stroke.

FIG. II.28. String Crossing on Open Strings

Scales

Practice this D major scale on the treble strings. When this pattern is comfortable, use scale patterns that are familiar to you. Extend the range by playing two- and three-octave scale patterns. Practice your dynamics, tone colors, and articulations. Use the techniques of both free and rest stroke.

FIG. II.29. String Crossing with a Scale

Composed Examples

6   7
Slow   A Tempo

Practice this example from "Variation 4" of "Chaconne" by S.L. Weiss. Pay attention to the fingerings for these short, ascending scale passages. Note the written articulations, and experiment with tone colors and dynamics. Notice that while, as a general rule, fingers should always alternate, there are instances in composed music that will call for repeated fingers. These instances often involve the addition of a bass note, or are in response to awkward string-crossings.

FIG. II.30. String Crossing in Single-Line Ascending Passage

8   9
Slow   A Tempo

Practice these scales from "Passacaglia" by S.L. Weiss. Pay attention to the fingerings for these short, descending scale passages.

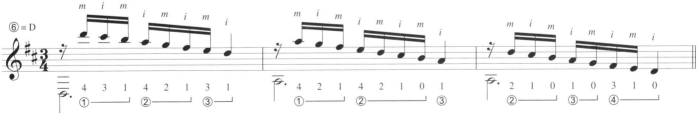

FIG. II.31. String Crossing in Single-Line Descending Passage

Alternation Between *p* and the Fingers

This covers the alternation between *p* and any combination of *i-m-a* played together. If you play in jazz or popular styles, you will find this technique useful for comping.

Place your hand into the basic position, with *p* planted on the fourth string and your fingers on the treble strings. Here's how the timing works: As the thumb plays and follows through, the fingers simultaneously plant on the treble strings. As the fingers play, the thumb simultaneously plants on its bass string. When you are practicing, it will appear that the motion of *p* plants the fingers, and the motion of the fingers plants *p*. Plant *p* and the fingers directly on the strings you wish them to play to sound the next note. Do not allow *p* or your fingers to anticipate the plant.

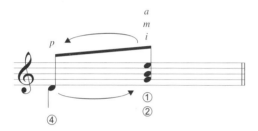

FIG. II.32. Alternation Between *p* and *i-m-a*

FIG. II.33. Alternating *p* and *i-m-a*

Practice

Away from the Guitar

Place your hand in the basic position, support your forearm, and "play" on your leg or a soft surface. This way, you can hear or feel your preparation/planting. Alternate *p* with *i-m-a* together, *p* with *i-m* together, *p* with *m* alone, and *p* with *i* alone. Remember, the only fingers that plant are the fingers you are playing. Make sure you follow through, and release tension when you do so. Your goal is for your motions to feel automatic and relaxed.

On Open Strings

Play the alternations from the previous exercises on open strings. As you are playing through the exercises, alternate the bass without deviating your hand position. Let your thumb reach for the fifth and sixth strings.

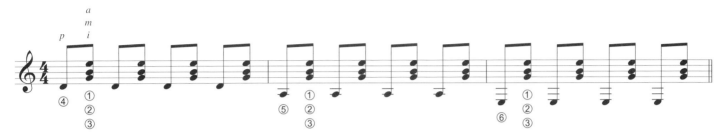

FIG. II.34. *p* and *i-m-a* Alternation on Open Strings

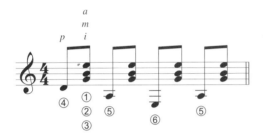

FIG. II.35. *p* and *i-m-a* Alternation on Open Strings with Alternating Bass

FIG. II.36. *p* and *i-m* Alternation on Open Strings

FIG. II.37. *p* and *i-m* Alternation on Open Strings with Alternating Bass

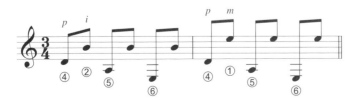

FIG. II.38. *p-i* and *p-m* Alternation on Open Strings

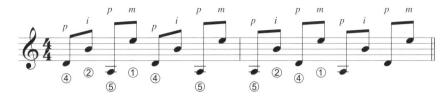

FIG. II.39. *p-i* and *p-m* Alternation on Open Strings and Different String Sets

Composed Examples

Practice this bass-line melody with alternating *i-m* together accompaniment. Make sure that *p* plants the fingers *only* when they are to play the following eighth note, and that the fingers plant *p only* when it is to play the next note. Concentrate your ear on the bass line to separate this voice and bring it out. Practice to connect the melody. Decide on your dynamics, tone colors, and articulations, and practice them.

10   11
Slow   A Tempo

FIG. II.40. *p* and *i-m* Alternation in a Musical Excerpt

Practice this excerpt from "Variation 6" of "Chaconne" by S.L. Weiss, focusing on your *p-m* and *p-i* arpeggios. Decide on your dynamics and articulations, and practice them.

12   13
Slow   A Tempo

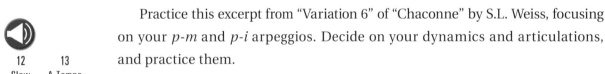

FIG. II.41. *p-m* and *p-i* Alternation in a Musical Excerpt

ARPEGGIOS

In classical guitar technique, an "arpeggio" is a right-hand fingerpicking pattern. Unlike in popular styles, the term "arpeggio" does not imply or require a specific chord voicing or left-hand fingering. There are three basic types of arpeggios, because (when you think about it) there are really only three more ways in which your fingers can move: in consecutive order from p to a, in order from a to p, or in a combination of the two. The following sections include the timing for each technique.

Full/Block Plant

In a full- or block-plant arpeggio, the thumb and fingers are played in order of strength, from strong to weak—for example: p, i, m, and a. The name "full" or "block" is used because the entire group of fingers to be played alternate with the thumb and plant on the strings together.

As a general rule in classical technique, stronger fingers are not planted on the strings while weaker fingers are playing. This can lead to tension in the hand and can diminish the amount of weight available for the playing finger's contact point. In this set of arpeggios, the stronger fingers always play first, so the fingers can plant as a block. Planting in this way relaxes the hand and allows for maximum power.

To practice timing, here are your steps for *p*, *i*, *m*, and *a*.

1. As *p* plays, the fingers are planted on the treble strings together.

2. *i* plays.

3. *m* plays.

4. As *a* plays, *p* is planted.

FIG. II.42. Full Block Plant: Alternating *p-i-m-a*

(a)   (b)

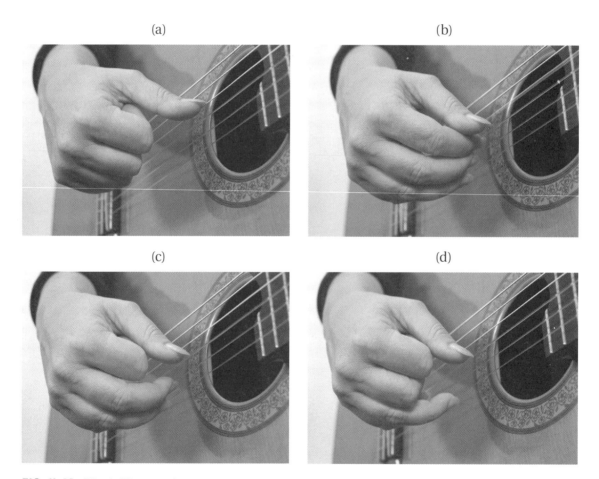

(c)   (d)

FIG. II.43. Block Plant: *p-i-m-a*

Rolling a Chord

Rolling a chord is a rapid block-plant arpeggio used to emphasize a chord. Many players use the slang "falling off the log" to describe the feeling of rapidly playing the thumb and each finger of the chord in anticipation and landing on the beat. As your last finger follows through, allow the weight of your hand and arm to pull your hand diagonally towards the floor. This will prevent your fingers from getting stuck on the strings.

If there is more than one bass string in the chord, you can incorporate a rest-stroke thumb into your roll. Adjust your hand position so that the entire plane of your thumbnail ramp is touching the lowest bass string in the chord. Sweep your thumbnail against each bass string. Play the highest bass string in the chord as a free stroke, and then "fall off the log" with your planted fingers.

Practice

Away from the Guitar

Place your hand in the basic position, support your forearm, and "play" on your leg or a soft surface. This way, you can hear or feel your preparation/planting. "Play" through the timing steps for *p-i-m-a*. Then "play" the timing steps for *p-i-m*. Make sure you follow through, and release tension when you do so. Your goal is for your motions to feel automatic and relaxed.

On Open Strings

Practice these block-plant arpeggios on open strings. As you are playing through the exercises, alternate the bass without deviating your hand position; let your thumb reach for the fifth and sixth strings.

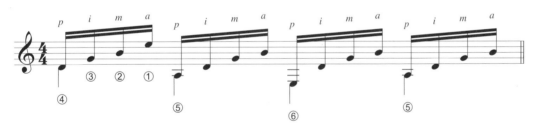

FIG. II.44. *p-i-m-a* Block-Plant Arpeggio on Open Strings

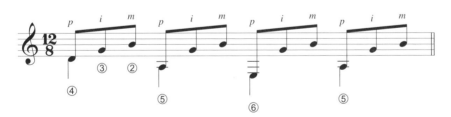

FIG. II.45. *p-i-m* Block-Plant Arpeggio on Open Strings

Composed Example

Practice this example with a *p-i-m* block-plant arpeggio. Concentrate your ear on the bass line to separate this voice and bring it out. Practice to connect the melody. Decide on your dynamics, colors, and articulations, and practice them.

14   15
Slow   A Tempo

FIG. II.46. *p-i-m* Block-Plant Arpeggio in a Musical Excerpt

Practice rolling the chords in this progression. Use the bass notes in parentheses to incorporate the rest-stroke thumb into your rolling technique.

16

FIG. II.47. Rolled Chords

Sympathetic-Plant Arpeggios and Tremolo

In sympathetic-plant arpeggios, your fingers play in order from weakest to strongest. The term "sympathetic" means that the act of playing one finger will plant the next finger. Remember, as a general rule, stronger fingers are not planted on the strings while weaker fingers are playing. This can lead to tension in the hand, diminish the amount of weight available for the playing finger's contact point, and, in the case of these arpeggios, it can trip you up.

It is most effective to practice your timing in these arpeggios beginning on the weakest finger and ending with your hand's strongest appendage, the thumb. Starting on the weakest finger in your practice will ensure that you support it properly in context. Because sympathetic preparation requires weaker fingers to set up stronger fingers, the method I use for this technique incorporates a "kick"—in which your thumb and/or index finger kicks a finger out a step early so that it is ready to be planted. Without the kicks, your sympathetic arpeggios can become lopsided or uneven in their timing.

Played in context with the thumb on alternating bass strings and the fingers playing a single treble string, this is the tremolo technique from the classical literature.

1. *a* plays and plants *m*
2. *m* plays and plants *i*
3. *i* plays, plants *p*, and kicks out *m* and *a* (as in your *i* and *m* alternation)
4. *p* plays, plants *a*, and kicks out *i* farther than *m**

*In step (4), *i* must kick out farther than *m* to ensure even timing. The more even the space between your *a*, *m*, and *i* fingers after a plant, the more even your arpeggio. (See the last photo in the sequence in figure II.49.)

FIG. II.48. *a-m-i-p* Arpeggio

Here is the timing for *a-m-i-p*.

(a) (b)

(c) (d)

(e)

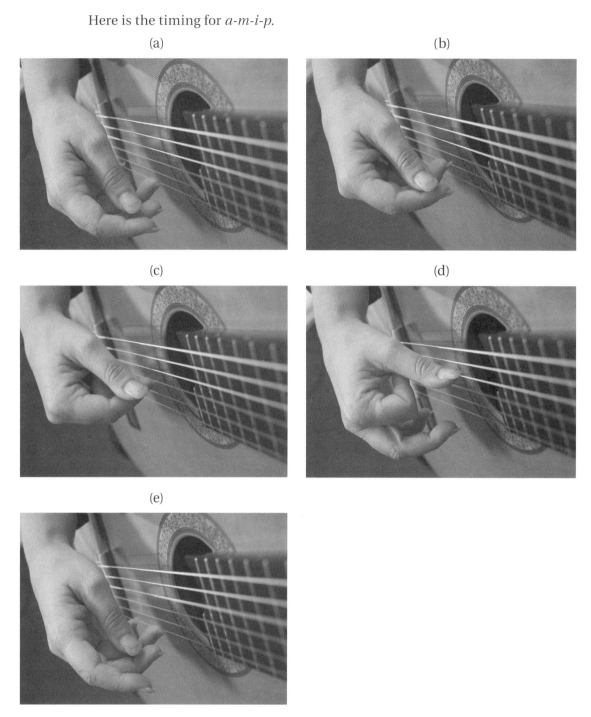

FIG. II.49. Sympathetic-Plant Arpeggio: *a-m-i-p*

Here is the timing for *m-i-p*.

1. *m* plays and plants *i*
2. *i* plays, kicks out *m* and plants *p*
3. *p* plays, kicks out *i* and plants *m*

Practice

Away from the Guitar

Place your hand in the basic position, support your forearm, and "play" on your leg or a soft surface. This way, you can hear or feel your preparation/planting. "Play" the timing steps for both of these arpeggios. Make sure you follow through, and release tension when you do so. Your goal is for your motions to feel automatic and relaxed.

On Open Strings

Practice the *a-m-i-p* arpeggio on four strings, alternating the bass from the fourth to the fifth and sixth strings.

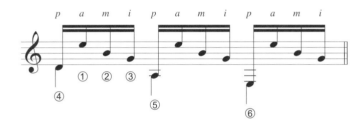

FIG. II.50. *a-m-i-p* Sympathetic-Plant Arpeggio on Open Strings

Practice this arpeggio as a tremolo, with the fingers playing on the first string and *p* alternating the bass from the fourth to the fifth, sixth, and third strings.

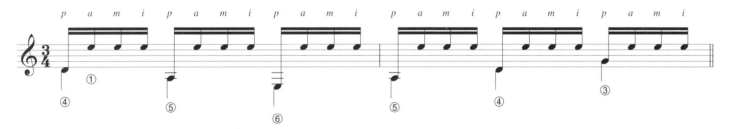

FIG. II.51. Tremolo on Open Strings

Composed Examples

Practice this sympathetic-plant arpeggio based on the chord progression from the "Theme" of "Chaconne" by S.L. Weiss. Decide on your dynamics, tone colors, and articulations, and practice them.

FIG. II.52. Sympathetic-Plant Arpeggio in a Musical Excerpt

Practice this tremolo example, inspired by the chord progression of "Chaconne" by S.L. Weiss. Decide on your dynamics and tone colors, and practice them.

FIG. II.53. Tremolo on a Musical Excerpt

Combination Arpeggios

Your repertoire will include arpeggio patterns that combine block- and sympathetic-plant techniques. In these "combination arpeggios," the steps for each arpeggio technique apply. Within the arpeggio, when the fingers are played in order from *p* to *a*, *p* plants the group. When the fingers are played in order from *a* to *p*, you will use sympathetic preparation.

FIG. II.54. Combination-Plant Arpeggio

Map out the timing in the examples here and in your repertoire. Practice them away from the guitar, on open strings, and in the context of the written excerpts.

Practice

On Open Strings

22   23
Slow   A Tempo

Practice the first part of this combination arpeggio, *p-i-m-a*, as a block plant, and the second part, *a-m-i-p*, as a sympathetic plant.

FIG. II.55. Combination-Plant Arpeggio in a Musical Excerpt

Practice this excerpt from "Variation 5" of "Chaconne" by S.L. Weiss. Map out the timing in this arpeggio: *p* and *m* together, *p-i-p-m-i-m-i-a-m-i*. Determine where you will use block planting and where you will use sympathetic planting.

FIG. II.56. Combination-Plant Arpeggio in a Musical Excerpt

PART III

The Left Hand

THE BASICS OF LEFT-HAND PLAYING

Finger	Fretboard Finger
Index, first finger	1
Middle, second finger	2
Ring, third finger	3
Pinky/Little, fourth finger	4
Open String (no finger)	0

As with the right hand, classical guitarists practice a basic left-hand position to facilitate accuracy, expressive potential, and facility without incorporating tension. This basic position calls for the fingers to be curved and to play on the fingertips, with the left-hand thumb *behind* the neck. This position provides the left hand with maximum leverage and facility, and balances the amount of weight available to each finger.

Classical players, who perform contrapuntal repertoire while negotiating a relatively wide-neck instrument and cylindrical nylon strings, will find this basic position to be a requirement. Shredders and bebop players often find this position useful as they practice for maximum velocity and consistency. Players in other styles, who are often called upon to fret and mute with their left-hand thumbs and use a flat-finger technique, will find plenty to steal from this classical left-hand concept. You can think of this position as a home base and deviate as necessary, or you can internalize the concepts as you think about your approach.

Basic Left-Hand Position

To find the basic left-hand position, hold your instrument in position and grab the neck of your guitar in 5th position (with your first finger at the 5th fret) like you're hanging off a tree-branch—with your fingers wrapped over the side, your palm pressed against the strings, and your thumb wrapped around the back of the neck. Now "roll up" your fingers and slide your thumb across the neck until all four of your fingers are resting on the sixth string on their fingertips. Look at your hand at this point and check that the following details are in place.

The part of the hand at which the fingers meet the palm is positioned parallel to the neck and slightly above the fretboard. On a wide-neck guitar, this part of your hand will be touching the first-string side of the neck while your fingers are placed on the sixth string. The left-hand thumb is positioned behind the neck (roughly behind the first and second fingers), resting on the pad of its unbent tip joint. This allows the fingers to reach across the strings and hold bass notes while simultaneously fretting treble notes. Your thumb's main job is balance. Instead of pushing up into the neck with your thumb, focus the weight of your whole arm down, using gravity to secure your position.

The general position of your fingers can be found by positioning them all on one string so that each finger gets a fret. The second and third fingers will be positioned "straight-on," while the first finger leans towards the head of guitar, and the fourth finger leans towards the body of the guitar.

 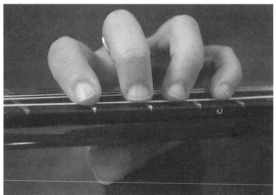

FIG. III.1. Left Hand

As the fingers cross the strings, the thumb moves across the neck horizontally *with* the hand, keeping the same position while string crossing. Likewise, when shifting up and down the strings, your thumb will move vertically with your hand. Don't forget to take your thumb with you!

Left-Hand Contact Points

As with your right-hand fingers, you will develop contact points with the fingers on your left hand. A consistent contact point will improve your accuracy and tone, and it will provide you with control over expressive tools.

To find your contact points on your left-hand fingers, place your hand into the basic left-hand position. Do this in fifth position on the guitar neck, with your fingers on the sixth string. Look at the way each fingertip contacts the string: your first finger will find its contact point on the thumb side of your hand, second finger in the center/slightly to the thumb side, third finger in the center/slightly to the pinky side, and your fourth finger on its far side. Apply pressure with all of your fingers, pressing the string onto the fingerboard. Now, release and relax your fingers, keeping them on the string. Repeat this several times. When you take your hand off the strings, the indentation the string has made in your fingertip is your contact point.

Now, try this one finger at a time. Hover your other fingers in position over the fret they will play, no more than a half-inch away from the fingerboard. Plant your first finger and push down; release the pressure and lift your finger from the string. Repeat this process with your other fingers. If your fingers seem to "fly away" from the fingerboard as they wait to "play," reconsider your basic left-hand position. Go slowly!

Practice

Left Hand Alone

In fifth position, "play" a 1-2-3-4 chromatic pattern on the sixth string. Vary the pattern: 1-3-2-4, 4-3-1-2. Cross strings and shift positions.

FIG. III.2. Left Hand Alone Chromatic Pattern

LEFT- AND RIGHT-HAND COORDINATION EXERCISES

Classical guitarists spend a lot of time coordinating their right- and left-hand fingers. If these motions are not in sync, your tone will be unclear, and you will sound as though you're playing with white noise in the background all the time. Coordination is an especially sensitive issue if you are new to right-hand technique but have extensively developed your left hand. On a basic level, your left hand must lead your right, securing the string before it is played by your right-hand finger. As you play your left- and right-hand fingers together, go slowly, feeling the contact point of each and the timing necessary to create a secure note with a full tone.

Practice

Play these chromatic scale patterns with *i* and *m* alternation in the right hand, and then again with *i* and *a* alternation. Develop these examples on one string and crossing strings, changing positions. Practice these examples on the bass strings, playing with *p*.

FIG. III.3. Chromatic Patterns for Left- and Right-Hand Coordination

Composed Examples

Use the composed examples from "The Thumb" and "Alternation" sections (in part II). Practice slowly, and concentrate on the timing between your hands.

Keep this "Coordination" section in mind when you play all of the examples in this book that incorporate both hands. Feel the contact point on your right- and left-hand fingers as they play. Memorize the feeling of physical security, and allow your ear to memorize the tone that accompanies that feeling. Continue to feel it out as you work in dynamics. As you are comfortable, you can increase the speed.

SLURS (HAMMER-ONS AND PULL-OFFS)

In classical technique, "ascending slurs" are the equivalent of hammer-ons in other styles. The main, subtle difference is that the hammer-on technique sounds more percussive than the classical ascending slur. Place your left hand in the basic position, with your first finger planted on the sixth string on the fifth fret. Place your right hand in basic position, and play the note with *p*. Quickly and decisively, bring your second finger down on its contact point on the fingerboard at the sixth fret. There is no need to "wind up," or raise your slurring finger higher than its hovering position, to produce a clear tone.

Descending slurs are the equivalent of pull-offs in other styles. Place your left hand in the basic position, with your first finger planted on the sixth string at the fifth fret and your second finger planted on the sixth string at the sixth fret. Place your right hand in basic position, and play the note with *p*. Slur with your second finger by pulling the string down across the fingerboard, as if you are playing it with your left-hand finger. A "pull-off" is essentially a "pull-down." This technique will produce the clearest tone. Resist the temptation to "pull up" with your slurring finger, as this will create a weak sound and take your finger too far away from the string.

Practice

Incorporate slurs into these chromatic exercises. Add ascending slurs (hammer-ons) to the ascending finger pairs, and descending slurs (pull-offs) to the descending finger pairs.

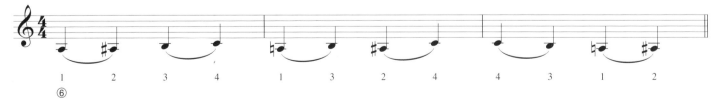

FIG. III.4. Chromatic Patterns with Slurs on a Single String

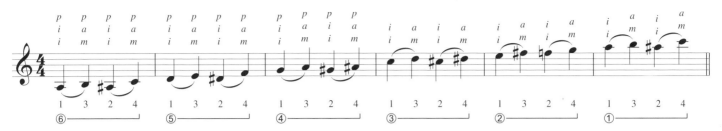

FIG. III.5. Chromatic Patterns with Slurs on All Strings

Composed Example

26

Play this example, and concentrate your ear on the slurs in the bass-line melody.
Connect the notes in the line using the slurs.

FIG. III.6. Ascending and Descending Slurs in a Melodic Excerpt

BARRE

Most guitar players have experience with left-hand barres. In the classical technique, there are three things to remember that will make your barres comfortable and your barred notes sound clear.

1. The first is your position: Classical players barre only with their first finger, because it is the strongest left-hand finger. When laying your first finger against a fret, place it as close to the fret bar as possible, and then roll slightly toward your thumb side so that the side of your finger presses on the strings.

2. Allow the weight you apply to the string to come more from the weight of your left arm hanging down off the neck, rather than pushing into the neck with your left-hand thumb.

3. Pay attention to the notes in the chord that need to sound under your first-finger barre. It is rare that all six strings will need to ring out, because other fingers will be fretting notes above the barre. Adjust the weight so that you are only pressing down the parts of your first finger that are sounding a note.

(a)   (b)

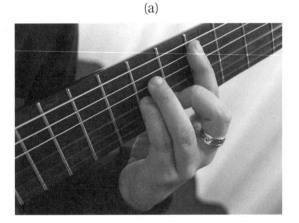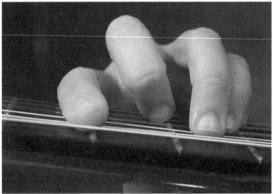

FIG. III.7. Barre Position

Practice

Composed Examples

Notice that in the first measure, your barre only has to sound the third and first strings. In measure 2, the second-half of the last beat, you'll barre five strings to sound only two and to set up for the next chord, which requires your barring finger to sound the fifth and third strings.

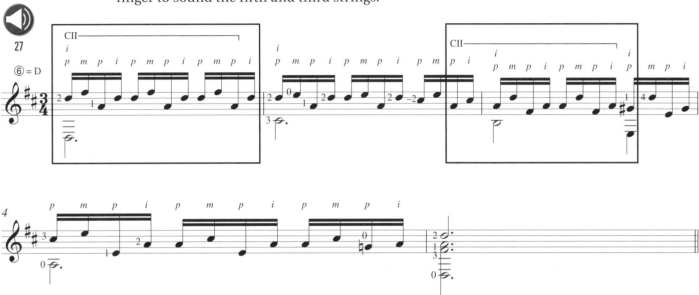

FIG. III.8. Barre in Measures 1 and 2–3

In this example, you don't need to set up your barre until measure 1, beat 2. Pay attention to the way you must prepare your left hand to make the arrival of this barre smooth.

FIG. III.9. Barre in Measure 1

VIBRATO

Most guitar players also have experience with vibrato. Vibrato is used to emphasize a note or create the illusion of elongated sustain. While each player develops his or her own expressive signature with vibrato, there are specific differences in the classical approach to this technique.

In classical technique, you create vibrato by planting your left-hand finger on a note, and then rocking your hand *vertically*. Your left-hand thumb will stay on the back of the guitar neck, rocking with your fretting finger. In this way, you pull the string slightly sharp and return it to pitch in rapid succession. The speed of your vibrato and when you begin it must be matched to the context of the piece you are playing. In many cases, you will begin the vibrato immediately after playing the note with your right hand. You'll start slowly and increase the speed, lightening up the pressure as the note dissipates.

In other styles, players create vibrato with other approaches—using a rapid, repetitive bending technique, or a circular motion with their fretting finger. These approaches will not sound stylistically authentic in classical music.

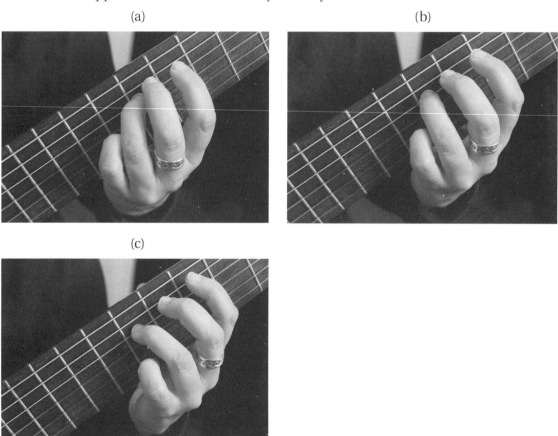

(a)　　　　　　　　　　　(b)

(c)

FIG. III.10. Vibrato

Practice

Using figure III.11, the "Theme" from "Chaconne," practice your vibrato. Choose notes from this melody to emphasize. Listen to the effect of this technique, and match the sound you desire with the feeling of accelerating the speed and changing the pressure of your left-hand fretting finger.

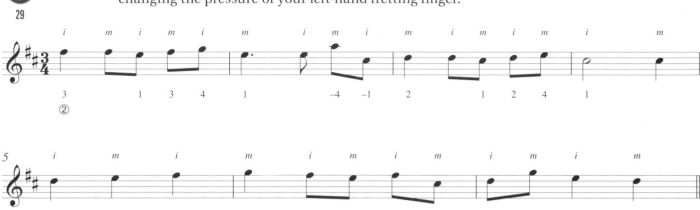

FIG. III.11. Vibrato on a Single-Line Melody

SHIFTING: FOUR TYPES

As your left hand shifts across and up/down the neck, you'll keep its basic position as consistent as possible. This will allow you maximum facility and the ability to connect the notes regardless of the space between them on the neck. In the classical technique, there are four general types of shifting. Identifying these types and practicing them will develop your left-hand accuracy and efficiency. In all of the shifts, be aware of your lift-off and arrival. Lift off gently, move decisively, and land gently. The more you choreograph your shifts, the more connected your playing will sound.

1. **Shapes (Horizontal and vertical):** In this type of shift, an entire chord shape is moved to a different place on the neck to fret the next notes. An example of a horizontal shape shift is the shift from an open E major chord to an open A minor chord. Vertical shape shifts move the same shape up and down the neck, as in figure III.12, measure 1, beat 3.

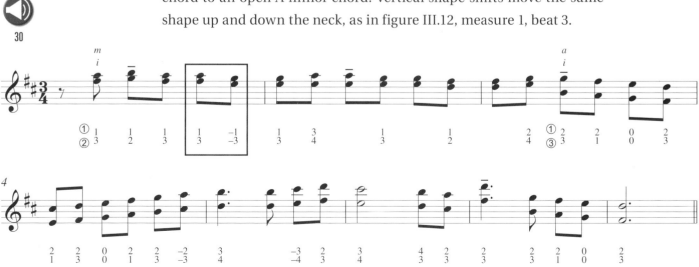

FIG. III.12. Shape Shift in Measure 1, Beat 3

2. **Pivot Shifts:** In this type of shift, one finger remains planted on a common tone between harmonies, while the left hand pivots to allow other fingers to play different notes. (See figure III.13, measure 1, beat 3 to measure 2, beat 1.)

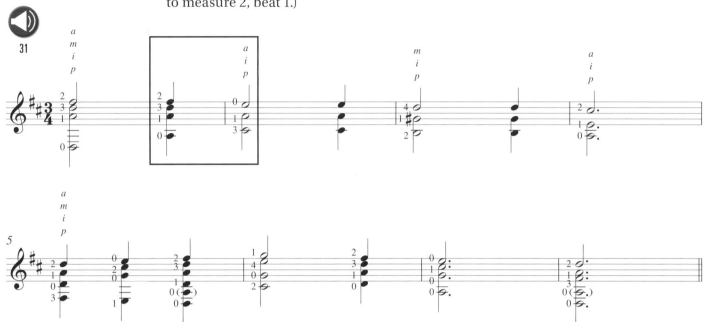

FIG. III.13. Pivot Shift in Measure 1, Beat 3 to Measure 2, Beat 1

3. **Guide Finger:** This type of shift occurs when your left-hand fingers move vertically on the neck between two different chord shapes that have at least one string in common. One left-hand finger will act as a guide, sliding lightly (not producing a sound) along the string—guiding the hand to the new position. In some instances, you can create a guide finger in a shift between shapes that do not share a common string.

In figure III.14, measure 3 beat 2 to beat 3, your fourth finger acts as a guide finger.

FIG. III.14. Guide-Finger Shift in Measure 3, Beats 2–3, Bass Line

In figure III.15, measure 7, beat 2 to beat 3, place your fourth finger on the fifth fret after playing the F♯ with finger 3, and immediately slide to B, creating a guide finger.

33

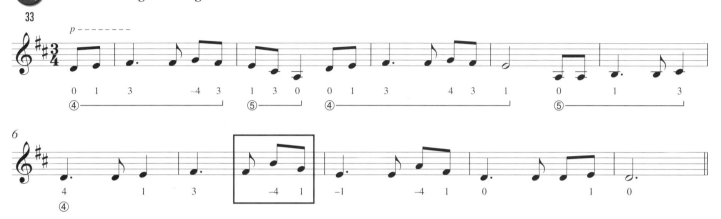

FIG. III.15. Created Guide in Measure 7, Beats 2–3

4. **Nothing in Common:** This is a shift between two completely different chords with no available pivots or guides. In these instances, make sure not to cut the duration of the first chord short. Then lift off, make the new shape in the air, and land gracefully. If interpretation allows, you can hold the melody note of the first chord after lifting the other fingers, allowing it to ring a moment longer before lift-off. This gives the illusion that there is no space created by the shift. Alternately, there are occasions in which you can plant the left-hand bass note or melody note of the second chord first, playing it and allowing it to ring while the rest of the chord is planted.

34

FIG. III.16. Nothing-in-Common Shift

PART IV

Warm-Up, Practice, Repertoire

WARM-UP ROUTINES

The examples presented throughout this book can be combined in a variety of ways and supplemented with excerpts from your repertoire to create warm-up routines. As I described in the "Introduction," I'm a big fan of practicing this way. Each day, I begin with general exercises to warm up my fingers, and add the basic techniques that target moments in my pieces. Here are a few routines that work for me. You can follow these as you develop your own.

Away from the Guitar

As I have my morning coffee, I run through all of these right-hand technique examples slowly, and away from my instrument.

1. Thumb push-ups
2. *i-m-a* together
3. Chords with *p* and the fingers played together
4. *i-m* alternation
5. Alternation between *p* and the fingers together
6. Block-plant arpeggio *p-i-m-a*
7. Sympathetic-plant arpeggio *a-m-i-p*
8. Combination arpeggio *p-i-m-a-m-i*

First Time on the Guitar for the Day

The first time I pick up the guitar, I do the following warm-up routine before diving into pieces in my repertoire or new works.

1. Right-hand techniques on open strings: Practice the "Away from the guitar" warm-up on open strings.

2. Left hand alone exercises.

3. Chromatic scale patterns, with left and right hands together, using *p* on the bass strings and *i-m* alternation on the treble strings. First playing every note, then incorporating slurs.

4. Composed and/or improvised examples that incorporate bass-string and treble-string melodies.

5. Excerpts from my repertoire that incorporate scales, and the corresponding examples in this book.

6. Excerpts from my repertoire that incorporate arpeggios, and the corresponding examples in this book.

7. Excerpts from my repertoire that incorporate challenging shifts, and the corresponding examples in this book.

Additional Practice Session Suggestions

Throughout the day, I begin each additional practice session by revisiting some of the basics. Briefly, I warm up with steps 3 and 4 from my "First Time on the Guitar for the Day" routine. Next, I repeat steps 5 through 7 with different excerpts from repertoire. Then, I practice a complete work from my repertoire.

REPERTOIRE: "CHACONNE" BY S.L. WEISS

Many of the "Composed Examples" in this book, and in my practice notebook, are excerpted from my transcription of the lute piece, "Chaconne" by S.L. Weiss (1686 to 1750).

35

As with all of the examples, incorporate dynamics, articulations, tone colors, and rolled chords into your interpretation. Write your choices into the score so that you can practice them consciously.

Chaconne

S.L. Weiss (1686–1750)
Transcribed by Kim Perlak

FIG. IV.1. "Chaconne" by S.L. Weiss

CONCLUDING THOUGHT

Technique is a set of tools. With relaxed hands and an understanding of the way they move, creative players harness their expressive power. I hope that this book has helped you add tools to your playing that give voice to your ideas. Best of luck in your music.

ABOUT THE AUTHOR

With performances that are deeply personal and express a breadth of tradition, guitarist Kim Perlak has been recognized as an inspired voice in American classical music. Her playing was praised by *The Austin American-Statesman* as, "thoughtful, enchanting, vivid…a songwriter's circle without the lyrics," and by another Austin reviewer as, "moving…the most patriotic thing I've experienced in many months."

Kim's versatile and inclusive approach to the instrument embraces new composition, education, and public service. Her performances of new classical works and collaborations with jazz and traditional players have been featured on National Public Radio, at the Yale Guitar Extravaganza, and at Boston GuitarFest. Her work combining performance, American music history, and outreach has been funded through grants from the Center for Southern African-American Music and Yale alumniVentures. Kim is the founder of the concert series "Ben & I Play for Peace," which supported the Veterans' Guitar Project-Austin, Wounded Warrior Project, and Wheelchairs for Iraqi Kids. This work was honored by the PBS program "From the Top" as part of their Arts Leadership series, and was recognized by the U.S. House of Representatives. From 2012 to 2015, Kim served as the editor-in-chief of *Soundboard, The Journal of the Guitar Foundation of America.*

Kim is the assistant chair of the Guitar Department at Berklee College of Music, where she has served in this position since 2013. She holds degrees from The University of Texas at Austin (DMA '08), Yale University School of Music (MM '01), and Stetson University (BM '98).

Kim plays guitars by Thomas Humphrey and Kirk Sand and endorses D'Addario Strings.

INDEX